Origin

Wild Space

Ally Kennen ■ Rayanne Vieira

OXFORD
UNIVERSITY PRESS

Chapter 1

Leo and Cassie lived in a space-house. It
had rocket-chimneys, a solar-door and a
star-garden, and it drifted round and round
Planet Earth.

Cassie and Leo were floating around the
kitchen. Cassie had switched off the gravity
machine. She liked being upside down.

Leo grabbed hold of the counter to stop himself floating up to the ceiling. "Switch the gravity back on, Cassie," he said. "I feel sick."

Leo didn't like floating about. He felt much better once the gravity was back on and he and Cassie were standing firmly on the floor. They both stared through the thick glass of the kitchen window.

"I can see a rocket coming towards us, but it doesn't look like Dad's rocket-bus," said Leo.

Cassie and Leo's family ran a space-safari business. People came up from Planet Earth to look at the strange animals living in deep space. Right now, their dad was out in space with his rocket-bus full of tourists.

Sometimes the children went with him, but today they had to do their homework. They'd been set a difficult task – to do something helpful – and they didn't have any ideas.

"I can't see any rockets," said Cassie. "Maybe you saw a comet-bird."

"No!" shouted Leo, excitedly. "It's not a comet-bird – it's Uncle Hunter's rocket!"

Uncle Hunter helped to run the space-safari because he was very good at finding new animals. The children watched as Hunter's rocket landed.

Just then, their mum came into the room. "Hunter wants to take you out," she said.

"Brilliant!" said the children.

"Well, you need to do your homework first," said Mum. "Don't you have to do something helpful?"

"But—" Cassie said.

"They can do it on the way," said Hunter, with a twinkle in his eye. "I can help them."

"OK," said Mum. "Just make sure you do."

"Great!" said Leo. "Where are we going, Uncle Hunter? I'd like to visit a baby star."

"I want to fly backwards around the Earth so fast we catch ourselves," said Cassie.

"That's impossible." said Leo.

"Where we're going is a surprise," said Hunter.

Chapter 2

Inside Hunter's rocket, Leo and Cassie strapped themselves into their seats. They both felt very excited. They always had fun with Hunter.

"We're off," said Hunter. Cassie and Leo waved at their mum through the window. She was in the star-garden, which twinkled and sparkled like sunlight on the sea on Planet Earth.

Hunter moved the controls and they zoomed into space. The rocket flew past stars and asteroids.

"Look," shouted Leo, "there's Dad!'

Dad was driving the space-safari rocket-bus through a field of stars. The children could see the tourists looking out of the windows as the rocket-bus whizzed past.

"He's coming back from Jupiter," said Cassie. "Lots of space creatures live there."

"Let's go to Jupiter!" said Leo. "I want to see the stone-cats and the giant dust-ants."

"We've seen them hundreds of times," said Cassie. "Where are we going, Hunter?"

"We're going to find something new," said Hunter.

Suddenly the rocket shuddered and shook. The engine made a funny noise.

"What's happening?" asked Leo.

"I'm not sure," said Hunter, frowning. He pressed the foot pedal and they flew more slowly. The engine was still making a strange noise.

"When will we be there?" asked Leo, feeling nervous.

"Now!" said Hunter. The rocket landed on the Moon with a gentle thud. Clouds of white dust rose up around them.

"But this isn't a surprise, it's the boring old Moon," said Cassie, unstrapping herself. "There are no animals on the Moon."

"Yes there are," said Hunter. "There are the moon-ponies."

The children felt disappointed. Everyone said the Moon was really boring. "Moon-ponies aren't *real*," Leo said. "They're just a story. Nothing lives on the Moon."

Chapter 3

They all got into their spacesuits and climbed out of the rocket.

The Moon was bare and empty, with nothing but dust and rocks and wide craters.

"Oh dear," said Hunter, looking at his rocket. "I need to fix this engine. You children go and look for the moon-ponies."

"You've got to be joking, Uncle Hunter," said Cassie. "Nothing lives on the Moon. The space-safari never bothers to land here."

Hunter smiled. "You're right. Nothing lives on the Moon. So why don't you look *in* the Moon?"

The children wandered off.

"He's wrong," said Leo. "I've never heard of a real moon-pony, and we have a space-safari business. Our family are experts in space animals."

"We might as well check," said Cassie. "Though it's hard to walk in these boots."

The children had heavy boots on so they didn't float away. There wasn't much gravity on the Moon.

"What did Hunter mean when he said 'look *in* the Moon'?" asked Leo. "How can we do that? It's just a giant rock."

"Look," said Cassie. She pointed at a big, wide crater. "Let's go over there."

The crater was very deep. The children slid down in their heavy boots. Down and down they went, till they reached a wide cave. They made their way towards it.

Chapter 4

There was a strange green light in the cave. The children kept walking. A shadow moved on the wall and they jumped.

"What's that?" whispered Leo. Cassie looked up.

There, drifting above them, was a tiny moon-pony. It was all white with little metal hooves. It was stuck against the top of the cave.

Cassie gasped. "Moon-ponies are real after all," she said. "Hunter was right."

"It can't get down," whispered Leo. "It's just a baby. It's too light. We have to rescue it."

Cassie took off one of her heavy boots and slowly rose up to the moon-pony.

"Be careful," said Leo.

"It's OK," said Cassie. "I'm good with no gravity. I like floating."

The moon-pony had eyes as black as deep space, with tiny stars in them. Its mane rippled in a gust of moon wind.

"Don't be scared," said Cassie. She put her arm around the moon-pony. They floated down. Leo grabbed Cassie's foot and pulled her to the ground.

Cassie put her boot back on and they walked with the moon-pony deeper into the cave.

After a while they came to a wide green underground lake. A group of moon-ponies were drinking from the water. The foal ran through the lake to its family.

The moon-ponies had huge silver hooves, like metal boots. They were whiter than the Moon. They all looked up at the children.

"*Wow*," said Cassie softly. "Wait till we tell Mum and Dad about this! I'm sure they've never seen a moon-pony! We can bring the space-safari down here to look at them."

"No," said Leo. "We should keep it secret and leave the moon-ponies in peace."

When they got back to the rocket, Hunter waved at them.

"Did you see anything?" he asked.

"This and that," said Leo.

"I'd rather not say," said Cassie.

Hunter smiled a secret sort of smile. "I've fixed the rocket. Let's go home."

When they got into their space-house,
Mum asked if they'd done their homework.

"Oh yes," said Leo, looking at Cassie out
of the corner of his eye. "We definitely did
our homework."

Alien animals

Scientists use telescopes and robots to look for animals on other planets and moons. They haven't found any yet!

We don't know if alien animals exist or what they might look like. They might be very small, or live in the water, or look like jellyfish. What do you think an alien animal might look like?